ChatOps
Managing Operations from Group Chat

Jason Hand

Beijing · Boston · Farnham · Sebastopol · Tokyo   **O'REILLY®**

ChatOps

by Jason Hand

Published by O'Reilly Media, Inc., 1005 Gravenstein Highway North, Sebastopol, CA 95472.

O'Reilly books may be purchased for educational, business, or sales promotional use. Online editions are also available for most titles (*http://safaribooksonline.com*). For more information, contact our corporate/institutional sales department: 800-998-9938 or *corporate@oreilly.com*.

Editors: Brian Anderson and Virginia Wilson
Production Editor: Kristen Brown
Copyeditor: Rachel Head
Interior Designer: David Futato
Cover Designer: Karen Montgomery
Illustrator: Rebecca Demarest

August 2016: First Edition

Revision History for the First Edition
2016-08-12: First Release

978-1-491-96230-5

[LSI]

Table of Contents

Foreword

Marc Andreessen famously opined that "Software is eating the world." His premise is that software companies are disrupting industry incumbents by outcompeting them as those industries increasingly deliver their value via online services—effectively, that all industries are moving online. This statement was a little bit controversial in 2011, but you'd be hard-pressed to find someone who disagrees with it in 2016.

These new companies are winning because they deliver a better experience to their customers and provide services faster and cheaper than the incumbents in their industries. Since their services are driven by software, they're able to apply the knowledge they gain from their own metrics, customer feedback, and market trends very quickly. Ultimately, they succeed because they've built organizations that are focused on collaboration and adaptability.

Over the last decade or so, the velocity at which applications are created, updated, and deployed has increased at an almost unbelievable rate. This acceleration is supported by significant improvements in the technology that we use to build applications and the processes we use to manage software development. I've been fortunate throughout my career to have been involved with a number of companies on the forefront of these changes.

I started working at 37signals (the creators of Basecamp and the Ruby on Rails application framework) in 2006, and saw firsthand how transformative Rails was in its ability to quickly deliver new applications and features. Since then, we've seen many of the ideas of early Rails adopted and expanded upon, and development velocity is now taken for granted. New applications frequently go from idea to minimum viable product in the span of weeks rather than months.

There have also been huge advancements in the infrastructure that supports these applications. I joined Heroku and later DigitalOcean because I believe in the vision that they both have for empowering developers to move quickly from idea to production deployment. The growth of cloud computing and the advancements in areas like configuration management, containerization, and orchestration (to name just a few), means that building physical infrastructure is no longer a barrier to delivering applications.

Later, when I worked at GitHub, our tagline was "Work better, together." This focus on collaboration is another cornerstone that enables the shift to a software economy. Development practices like Agile, which emphasizes collaboration between developers and product stakeholders, have become the norm. Text chat, which was once reserved for engineers talking to one another, is becoming a primary communication channel for more and more companies.

We've seen tremendous improvements in our ability to quickly and cheaply build and deploy applications, but our ability to manage these applications after deployment has not advanced as rapidly. Many organizations have learned a tough lesson: our previous models of IT, particularly the focus on mitigating risk rather than delivering value, can be debilitating to our ability to move quickly.

Over the last few years we've seen the DevOps movement emerge, with the goal of improving collaboration between software development and operations and an emphasis on automation. Organizations that embrace DevOps nearly universally report improvements to their deployment processes and increased ability to quickly deliver new applications and features. In many cases, though, even DevOps implementations don't go far enough and the collaboration stops once an application is deployed. Organizations often fall back on more traditionally siloed IT operations practices around issues like incident management, troubleshooting, and remediation.

ChatOps delivers on the promise of collaboration that the DevOps movement promotes, and extends it throughout the entire lifecycle of the application. It brings the workflows that your teams already use when building, deploying, and managing applications and infrastructure to the place that your organization already collaborates—your chat client.

At GitHub, we were on the leading edge of this movement and nearly every technical interaction could be driven from and collaborated on directly in chat. For example:

- Software and operations engineers could deploy applications, balance storage clusters, mitigate DDoS attacks, and more.
- The support team could investigate, and often even resolve, customer problems.
- Product managers could review metrics to understand usage of features to make prioritization decisions.

The value of visibility in terms of shared context is obvious, but there are a number of other benefits. Instead of teaching a new developer how to deploy applications or referring them to documentation that is invariably out of date, they can see how deployments happen on their first day. Product managers don't have to ask if a new feature has been deployed yet, because they can see when it happens for themselves.

Jason has been at the vanguard of the ChatOps movement for years, and his excitement about the topic is infectious. He combines a technical background that allows him to understand the details with a broader industry view, thanks to frequent interaction with VictorOps customers and the DevOps community. This report does a great job of setting the stage by describing why ChatOps is important, illustrating how it fits within organizations, and explaining the factors that you should consider as you start your own adoption journey.

I believe, like Marc Andreessen, that software is eating the world. Organizations that collaborate better and adapt faster are well positioned to take advantage of this trend; collaboration and adaptability are what ChatOps is all about.

— Mark Imbriaco
Founder of Operable
Cog ChatOps Platform
August 2016

CHAPTER 1

Introduction

In recent years, there has been a movement within organizations to become much more collaborative and open when it comes to communicating about efforts, concerns, and projects, especially across multiple teams and departments. When organizations place a high focus on sharing more about what takes place throughout the day in an environment that is accessible by all, higher efficiencies can be achieved in a number of areas. Finding ways to increase the speed and velocity of delivering software and services to end users is of the utmost importance to all modern IT departments, but finding new ways to accomplish our daily tasks more efficiently is something *all* departments within an organization are examining.

Popular group chat tools such as Slack and HipChat have allowed for greater transparency about what goes on throughout the day within teams and organizations. By engaging in conversations in a shared space where others can be part of the discussion, greater awareness and efficiencies are provided to a larger part of the team. Important information and discussions are shared and made available across entire teams and organizations. Rather than artificially blackboxing that information in one-on-one emails or instant messages, it is disseminated to others, allowing for well-informed and high-performing teams to take shape, as well as helping to drive innovation within the company.

What Is ChatOps?

ChatOps is about using group chat tools to go beyond basic conversation, juxtaposing discussion with context and actions taken from within the chat tool itself. By creating a unified interface for teams to take action, view relevant information, and discuss all of it in line with each other, ChatOps allows many benefits to be gained across teams and organizations.

The goal of this report is to outline the benefits of ChatOps, as well as concerns organizations and teams should consider as they begin to roll out their own ChatOps efforts. I'll touch on some of the existing technology available today as well as how teams are using persistent group chat, third-party (native) chat integrations, and chatbots to provide even more functionality and capabilities for teams managing varying aspects of IT operations and beyond.

Those who are considering their own ChatOps journeys and looking to consume a high-level rundown of what is necessary to begin should find the contents of this text a good starting point. Very little of the text will be technical in nature. The important concepts of ChatOps are not difficult to understand, nor are they unique to any specific tool, framework, or programming language.

Facilitating a culture of increased sharing, shortened feedback loops, automation of tasks, and cross-functional teams, ChatOps has been central to many organizations as they begin to evolve toward a DevOps model.

Throughout the report, I'll cover some of the key concepts and technologies that have emerged in recent years, in addition to the challenges that one must consider. These ideas will set the stage for you and your team or organization to begin planning out your own ChatOps efforts, as well as providing the language needed to discuss the potential benefits and concerns with leadership.

What's in the Report

I think it's important to point out that a ChatOps approach requires a change in your company's culture. I want to start off by discussing that specific challenge in Chapter 2. By understanding the key benefits associated with ChatOps, you and your team will begin to find the language to use with senior management to win their endorsement. Examining benefits such as increased collaboration, dissolving blackboxed conversations, and creating high-performing and cross-functional teams will be the primary focus of Chapters 3 and 4. Then we will take a look at some of the common use cases of ChatOps and the technology behind them in Chapters 5, 6, and 7. We'll round out the report by discussing more of the nuanced topics behind ChatOps in Chapters 8 through 15. Security concerns, managing a good "signal-to-noise" ratio, and what to think about when relying on third-party chat services are just a few of the things we'll take a closer look at.

What's Not in the Report

The majority of this report focuses on the "why" of ChatOps. Because so much of the "how" depends on the technology you select, I won't be covering technical aspects such as hosting and configuring any of the group chat tools or chatbots mentioned in the coming chapters. The step-by-step procedures vary from tool to tool and are beyond the scope of this report. Getting everything up and running shouldn't be much of a challenge, but fortunately every tool that I highlight in Chapter 6 has great documentation and a growing community to leverage for technical assistance if you run into problems.

The Author

At VictorOps, I have led the adoption efforts of ChatOps internally. For more than two years, the underlying concepts have often been at the forefront of my responsibilities and efforts. Users of our "on-call and incident management service" are early adopters of ChatOps, whether they are aware of the concept or not. Acknowledging, triaging, investigating, and resolving incidents from the VictorOps interface or from a group chat tool via an API is a perfect use case of ChatOps. Sharing information, taking action to address service disruptions, and continuously improving are the byproducts and are why I've grown passionate about the topic of ChatOps.

My intent is that by the completion of this report you'll have a really good starting point to begin your own ChatOps journey and explore the new levels of efficiency and other benefits it can offer your team, your organization, and the products and services you provide.

CHAPTER 2

The Culture Challenge

Many of the principles and concepts that have come out of the DevOps conversation require organizations to examine their own company culture and approach to work. ChatOps, a concept born from the DevOps movement, is no exception to this. However, the return on investment of ChatOps coupled with the broader benefits that evolve as a byproduct are immediate and measurable.

Benefits of ChatOps

The benefits of ChatOps can be broken down into two categories: social and technical. Varying members of your team and organization are going to be attracted to some benefits over others. Management and members of non-technical teams may find the social benefits reason enough to begin the journey.

NOTE

Social Benefits

- Increased collaboration
- Increased sharing of domain knowledge
- Increased visibility and awareness
- Enhanced learning
- Improved empathy

Engineers and members of technical teams within an organization will likely find greater value in the technical benefits. These more closely address the concerns they are faced with on a day-to-day basis.

Technical Benefits

- Increased automation
- Increased speed of actions and executed commands
- Improved security and safety
- Automatic logging of conversations and actions
- Synchronous communication
- Reduction in email

Identification of these benefits has led many who are beginning to take notice of the success that DevOps has brought organizations to look to ChatOps as a starting point. At its core, ChatOps is primarily about increased sharing and collaboration regarding efforts and actions taken each day. A higher focus on collaboration, automation, context, and shared institutional knowledge is at the heart of what DevOps has brought to teams and organizations.

With very little effort, teams that begin to move their conversations out of email and private messages and into persistent group chat tools (coupled with powerful chatbots and third-party integrations) begin to see the benefits outlined above. As a result, the organization begins to evolve into one that is efficient in its actions and inherently good at knowledge sharing. On top of that, previous friction in the path toward adoption of DevOps may be a result of not knowing where to start. As teams and management begin to see what automating simple tasks from within group chat can do for them, teams, departments, and entire organizations are able to begin focusing more effort on improvements. It's through that line of reasoning that real learning and innovation begin to emerge.

Champion of Change

Every organization has its own unique culture, and the larger the company is, the harder it is to change. Through adoption of ChatOps techniques, teams will begin to see incremental improvements toward the culture they seek. It's not easy, and it will take time. But including more and more individuals and teams in conversations has a way of peeling away the bureaucracy and old-view thinking that typically prevents any real change in a company's culture. Perhaps most importantly, every significant change in the culture of an organization needs a champion. Someone who takes the lead to be an agent of change. As demonstrated by your interest in this report, it is highly likely that the champion is you.

 NOTE

ChatOps Helps to Facilitate:

- Increased sharing
- Shorter feedback loops
- Automation of tasks
- Cross-functional and high-performing teams

CHAPTER 3

Team Collaboration

ChatOps is about increased sharing and collaboration regarding efforts and actions each day. Common across many organizations, while also unique to your own internal environment and processes, the specific actions that teams collaborate and execute on will vary. In Chapter 5, I'll outline some of the common actions many teams are currently using to automate sharing of important information or executing commands. I will also begin touching on more technical considerations of ChatOps. Regardless of which actions you implement, by placing a higher focus on open and shared conversations, paired with related context, command execution access, and increased awareness of all of it, you will find greater efficiencies across the board.

All of Us Are Smarter than Any of Us

Innovation is the result of combining and recombining ideas over and over. When collaboration occurs frequently and involves more and more individuals, a great deal of learning and innovation are realized.

Artificial siloing of teams begins to dissolve as institutional knowledge is made available to a broader part of the organization. Increased transparency and conversations that are open to all voices lead to highly efficient, cross-functional teams. Teams are enabled to learn from one another. We want to create as many ideas as possible, and as a result, brainstorming is encouraged. Good brainstorming exercises are those built on other ideas from a diverse range of voices and expertise in an environment where all members can be heard.

Brainstorming Tip

Good brainstorming efforts avoid the opportunity for "group think." The more diverse and varying ideas that make their way into the conversation, the better the results of a brainstorming exercise will be. By allowing teams to engage in conversations intended for brainstorming new ideas, group chat tools provide an environment for individuals to share their own viewpoints and ideas. Those who may struggle to share or speak up in physical meetings will be more inclined to participate in brainstorming sessions from the abstracted comfort of a chat room.

Don't Repeat Yourself

It is through this behavior that a team understands what is happening throughout its codebase, infrastructure, and company. A deeper understanding of what is happening and what has already taken place means a team won't take the next logical step along an unproductive path. Because information, actions, and context is shared and visible for all to see, duplication of efforts can be avoided. Individuals and teams will find that the shared conversations provide insight into what has already been done, what needs to be done next, and what lessons have been learned by those already taking action.

An increase in collaboration is the most immediate positive benefit from a ChatOps effort. This new approach to collaboration speaks to the evolving roles of engineers within IT departments and beyond.

CHAPTER 4

Roles and Responsibilities of DevOps (or Ops) Engineers

Until recent years, the roles and responsibilities of IT teams were made very specific and clear. However, through Agile software development and DevOps, cross-functional teams are beginning to demonstrate the effectiveness of tearing down the traditional divisions of labor. By making collaboration a priority, team members are beginning to understand more than just their own unique roles within their teams and organizations. Empathy between teammates and even different teams begins to take hold, and a sense of ownership and accountability becomes central to all actions. That empathy then bleeds over into the designing of services (both software and infrastructure), and the end users' needs are given the utmost consideration for all business decisions.

Build Empathy

Should your organization make the unfortunate decision that teams should remain isolated and task-specific, ChatOps still helps to create greater empathy within the teams.

The visibility of work as it takes place helps to create a shared context and understanding both within and across individual teams. It's easier to accept that your own request cannot be completed immediately when you have visibility into the work of others.

Goal Alignment

In previous software development and IT efforts, goals often varied from one department to the next. Software developers were incentivized and rewarded for meeting metrics typically tied to quantity of code "shipped." IT Operations teams were incentivized for preventing outages, and their primary efforts centered around providing maximum uptime of service to both internal and external stakeholders or customers. Likewise, Security, Network, Database, Support, and every other breakout team within Information Technology all had their own concerns, goals, and efforts associated with accomplishing their objectives. The problem was that rarely did these goals align in a way that placed the needs of the end user and business as the top priority.

Now, organizations are beginning to see the measurable gains made possible by creating highly efficient, cross-functional teams where more of the team members are enabled. For example, rather than just the IT Operations subgroup assuming the responsibility of being "on call" for service disruptions, more members of the team (including developers and even management) are taking on this responsibility. After all, they have intimate knowledge of and expertise on subject matter that could be directly related to problems. More of the team can also be part of the planning, design, building, and maintenance of software and the infrastructure on which it resides.

Spreading Institutional Knowledge

A key component of these cross-functional teams is their ability to collaborate effectively. By moving many of their conversations, as well as records of actions and context, into a persistent group chat tool, friction that previously caused delays in the development, maintenance, and support of software and infrastructure is removed. Institutional knowledge and awareness of many aspects within IT and beyond are given the opportunity to persist and grow over time. Live documentation on exactly how things are accomplished is generated as it's happening.

Live Documentation

Utilizing ChatOps is a great way of onboarding new team members. Documentation on "how jobs get done" is available in real time for all to see. By viewing the conversations, actions, and more from within a group chat tool, individuals can quickly learn how to accomplish a great deal of work.

Documentation is and has always been an incredibly important part of every role within IT. Keeping documentation up-to-date means that teams always have the most accurate information available to them. ChatOps provides a natural method of automatically and persistently maintaining up-to-date documentation. At any time, personnel can review conversations and actions from within group chat to consume the most recent information with regard to current status and procedures to accomplish a growing number of tasks.

Learning Organization

The role of IT Ops engineers is often consumed with efforts toward prediction and prevention of service disruptions. ChatOps enables a focus on sharing information, learning, improving, and innovating to make services more resilient and reliable. The same focus on learning should apply to all roles within IT.

Spreading the load and knowledge across larger groups and teams affords deeper understanding and learning. This in turn provides opportunities to experiment and innovate on the processes and tools of both software engineers and those who were previously labeled as IT engineers or system administrators. Much of this comes directly as a result of treating persistent group chat as the common interface for nearly everything that takes place within the team.

In the following chapter, I'll begin to outline some of the ways teams are leveraging ChatOps in their own organizations to increase awareness, simplify tasks, increase velocity, and more.

CHAPTER 5

Common Uses and Tasks

Much of what ChatOps provides teams and organizations is a common interface to interact with a growing number of services and tools. The benefits are clear, and with minimal effort, automation of tasks (while preserving the conversations and context related to them) can provide a great deal of value to not only the operators executing commands and discussing the results, but additional stakeholders as they review the timeline of events.

Aside from querying the weather or sharing random GIFs, what can be done that brings immediate value to our teams and the business? In this chapter, we'll break tasks down into several categories and discuss examples of what teams are currently doing with ChatOps.

Pushing Context

The easiest and therefore first step that many take on the path to ChatOps is simply pushing additional context about events or actions into the conversations. Without good context, team members don't have the full picture of previous and present conditions. It's through extra and ongoing context that teams remain aware of situations as best they can, shortening feedback loops and facilitating quicker responses.

Many services that we use on a regular basis are able to "push" data to modern chat clients in a variety of ways. Through the use of webhooks or RESTful endpoints, chat clients can ingest data seamlessly and with very little setup. The result is that as an event takes place somewhere outside of the natural bounds of awareness, information is passed along to the chat client for all to see and know about.

 Example Notifications

- Infrastructure creation notifications
- Anomaly, incident, and outage notifications
- New or updated support tickets
- Version control repository changes
- Event or meeting reminders
- Social media engagement

As commits, pull requests, and additional actions are taken within your team or company's repository, information about those actions is automatically pushed to a specific channel or room within the chat client. This means when a developer executes a command to commit new code to a repository, for example, that information is instantly shared with others on the team. Note that in this example the developer does not commit the code from chat. That action is taken elsewhere, likely from the developer's own machine. The results, however, are immediately shared with everyone on the team via the group chat tool.

"Read-Only" Retrieval of Data

For many teams, an early use is to set up the ability to query services or databases in a safe manner. Providing a safe way for team members to retrieve information from a datastore without the risk of manipulating data means that a broader group of people can have deeper visibility into the data. By enabling people who do not (and should not) have access to query databases from a command-line or other tool to look at the data without bothering a person who does have that access, you empower your team in a way that brings a great deal of efficiency and knowledge sharing to the table.

Example Queries

- CRM records

- Open incidents and on-call schedule in VictorOps or PagerDuty

- Graphite or DataDog graphs

- Log data

- DNS and WHOIS records

- Infrastructure databases

It's not uncommon for members of a non-technical team to have questions about data that typically only members of the technical team have access to. Compliance controls and regulations are put in place to prevent unauthorized access to sensitive data. However, some of that data is very relevant and helpful to those who don't have access to query a database containing that data directly. Enabling "read-only" retrieval of data from within a group chat client allows those from non-technical teams to obtain the information that they need without interrupting someone who has access. Users can simply type a specific string of commands and, through the use of a chatbot, obtain the information that they need in a safe manner, without having to ask someone from the technical team to do it for them. Additionally, others who may view the timeline can see who queried the database, what the results were, and how it was done. Documentation on how to obtain that type of information is built in real time and an audit trail is generated as well.

Bidirectional Interactions

Pushing context and querying data are where many teams first start exploring the possibilities of ChatOps. At some point, however, deeper interactions will be desired or required. This is where more advanced bidirectional interactions with services and tools prove their usefulness.

NOTE

Example Two-Way Interactions

- Manage incident notifications in VictorOps or PagerDuty
- Manage a project board in Trello
- Facilitate daily "stand-up" meetings
- Shorten URLs using Bitly or Google's URL shortener
- Perform language translations using Google Translate
- Poll groups
- Save and retrieve bookmarks

Third-Party Integrations

Most of the popular group chat tools discussed in the next chapter provide some type of "app directory," allowing an easy method to connect and configure third-party tools and services. The use of these integrations avoids the need of a bot, as the third-party service connects directly to your chat application.

The upside of this approach is that it's extremely easy to integrate applications as well as manage them. Non-technical team members can browse the growing list of services and select the ones that they use. In most cases, an admin user of the company or team's chat application will need to authorize the integration, but it's typically as simple as clicking a few buttons.

The downside is that customization of how to interact with the service and how the data is returned is limited. In many cases this is not a deal-breaker, but some teams prefer to customize their interactions with the third-party tool or service. In those cases, using a chatbot (and the associated development) is required. Nevertheless, many teams set up these integrations as an easy way to get started down the path of ChatOps. Both HipChat and Slack make it easy to turn on, try out, and turn off integrations with very little effort. This allows teams the ability to explore simple interactions with the tools and services they use without having to dedicate technical resources to their efforts.

NOTE

Native Third-Party Integration Examples

- Create Google Hangouts
- Create Calendar events
- Share Google Drive documents
- Share Dropbox documents
- Interact with Salesforce
- Receive pull requests, commits, and comments in BitBucket and GitHub
- Create, manage, and close Wunderlist to-do lists
- Interact with support ticketing systems such as Zendesk and Desk.com
- Create and update status pages

Custom Scripted Tasks

One of the most powerful aspects of ChatOps is the ability to daisy-chain actions together. In other words, separate actions can be automated individually, then those separate actions can be processed in a specific sequence. In many cases information returned from the first action will be used to decide the next step of the process. This, however, requires the use of a chatbot as it steps through multiple actions within a script or library of scripts. For many actions taken from within a group chat tool, a simple call and response is all that is desired. In others, we just want the context provided to us automatically and in real time. But there are many circumstances where interactions with services need to be stepped through in sequence and with different services or tools. In those cases, scripted tasks can be executed through the use of a chatbot.

The instructions that your chatbot will execute contain all of the actions in a specific order. They also contain the necessary application programming interface (API) calls and authorization information required to trigger the actions. Everything is executed in a specific order. If a certain amount of time is required to pass before the next step is executed, that "wait" syntax is included in the instructions. If certain information is required for a step to take place, a previous step will query a service and provide that information so that the sequential steps can execute once it has the information it requires.

Custom Script Examples

- Updating configuration files
- Submitting a support ticket to an outside service (such as an internet service provider)
- Two-factor authentication
- Infrastructure provisioning and configuration management operations
- Database migrations
- Managing Lightweight Directory Access Protocol (LDAP) servers
- Managing virtual private networks (VPNs)

Now that we have an idea of the types of actions and context that can be provided, let's examine some of the existing technology that teams and organizations are currently leveraging.

CHAPTER 6

Existing Technology

While the term may be new to many, the concepts and technology behind ChatOps have been around for quite some time. Persistent group chat has long existed in a variety of forms. Chatbots, while suddenly a hot topic, have been part of IT's arsenal for many years. For some, much of what you will find in this text may not sound all that different from what you were doing using Internet Relay Chat (IRC) many years ago. As with any technology, however, there have been advancements and evolution within our tools and the ways that we can utilize them. The concepts of ChatOps are not unique to any one specific chat client or chatbot. However, understanding what teams are currently using for their own ChatOps efforts may help you frame where to start. Learning about existing technology and what can be accomplished with it will help you form ideas and provide a starting point for you and your team.

Chat Services

While persistent group chat has existed for quite some time and IRC has been a staple of IT culture for many years, it wasn't until more recently that modern group chat tools began to evolve into something much more user-friendly and valuable to a larger group of users in the organization. 37signals's Campfire application was one of the first to provide much of the same functionality as IRC, but with a cleaner and more user-friendly design. Additionally, the ability to integrate third-party services and leverage APIs opened the door to much more for teams to explore. When the term "ChatOps" was coined by the team at GitHub in 2011, Campfire (*https://campfir enow.com/*) was the persistent group chat tool used at the time. While it's still a popular option, let's take a quick look at some of the alternatives.

HipChat

Atlassian's HipChat (*https://hipchat.com/*) has gained popularity in recent years. Its seamless integration with additional tools from the Atlassian suite makes it extremely easy for teams to begin interacting and sharing context from multiple tools and services from within their own persistent chat client. By providing an open market for developers and tech companies to show off their own native integrations with HipChat, Atlassian also makes it possible for teams to find more tools outside of its suite to leverage from within the chat client.

Atlassian has since released HipChat Server, an on-premise solution for organizations that want to leverage group chat, regardless of their ChatOps aspirations. Using a hosted chat solution has been one of the largest barriers to entry for many organizations looking to provide more collaboration, transparency, and efficiency. More recently, Atlassian has released HipChat Connect, the latest incarnation of its group chat product. With this release, a focus has been placed on deeper integrations with third-party services and tools to provide even more functionality to HipChat users. It also provides a "Glance" feature that allows team members to review what they may have missed since they last used the tool. A high-level summary of conversations, context, and actions is displayed in a separate pane, making it easier for team members to get caught up and gain the awareness they need without having to constantly be tuned into the conversations taking place. This goes a long way in helping to deal with noise and alert fatigue and is an attractive feature to management, who may not tune into the chat so often.

Flowdock

Rally Software (now CA Technologies) acquired Flowdock (*https:// www.flowdock.com/*) in 2013. Much like HipChat, Flowdock seamlessly integrates with the Rally product line, allowing teams to have better awareness of and visibility into their data from the comfort of their chat client. One of the biggest differentiators of Flowdock is its ability to thread conversations. Despite efforts to maintain a sterile room or channel and ensure that conversations stay on topic, multiple lines of thought or sub-conversations naturally develop over time. Many people can be in one room or channel discussing topics that are relevant to the overall theme of the room, but there will likely be different subthreads. It's often hard to come back to a conversation and provide extra context or valuable information to the conversation if others have moved on to a new topic. Threading allows for teams to keep specific conversations linked to one another so that those who may review the conversations later have a better understanding of how everything is related.

Slack

Slack (*https://slack.com/*) has generated an immense amount of attention and admiration from teams large and small. Its user interface (UI) and user experience (UX), including a quirky onboarding experience for new users, have been the primary selling point for many. Functionally, Slack provides the same features as nearly all other persistent group chat tools on the market. The design aspects have primarily been what has won over its customers from the competition. Much like other tools, Slack provides an open market full of third-party integrations and hosted chatbots that can be integrated in with just a few clicks, providing even more functionality to teams with very little lifting or the need for technical staff to be involved beyond simply authorizing an integration. The built-in "Slackbot" comes baked in with a number of useful actions it can take on behalf of a user. With nearly two million daily active users, Slack has caught the attention of not only large businesses and startups, but just about any type of community you can think of.

Additional Open Source and Commercial Options

Additional group chat tools and services, some of which are open source projects, are gaining in popularity as well. Grape, Zulip, Rocket, Gitter, Grove, and Mattermost are just a few alternatives to the group chat services mentioned above. The primary thing to consider when evaluating a group chat client is its ability to integrate with a chatbot or its support for native integrations with third-party services. Any chat tool that does not allow for interactions with services will not provide the essential elements of ChatOps. A collaborative environment where teams can discuss topics is just the beginning. Being able to interact with more and more of the tools and services that we use in our daily tasks is where the power of ChatOps becomes much more apparent.

Third-Party Integrations

All of the popular group chat tools outlined previously have a vast market of integrations and hosted bots that allow teams to begin setting up their ChatOps efforts with very little trouble (Figure 6-1). The popularity of HipChat and Slack has drawn the attention of developers as well as Software as a Service (SaaS) companies that want to make it easy for their users to interact with their services from within chat. The marketplace is divided into categories, making it fairly easy to browse and search for specific services or functionality. As more and more non-technical teams join the ChatOps conversation, even more integrations are showing up in the market for teams to integrate and leverage.

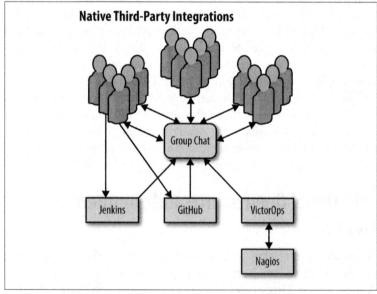

Figure 6-1. Using native third-party integrations

Through the use of third-party integrations, teams are able to begin interacting with the tools and services that they use each day without the need for a chatbot. This makes the barrier to entry for

ChatOps much lower for teams that don't have the bandwidth or technical expertise to set up and configure their own chatbots. Additionally, development of those integrations is handled by the services and updates to functionality can be expected to remain consistent. Support is available from the service providers as well, making it much less of a burden on a technical team to manage and support not only the bots but the definitions and instructions that are required for the chatbots to interact with outside services.

Bots

Although many teams may not need to host, configure, and support a chatbot, as a team's ChatOps efforts get more advanced it may find that third-party integrations do not provide the full functionality or customization that it requires. It's at this point that a chatbot may become necessary to fully realize the capabilities of ChatOps and allow teams to manage the interactions with tools and services in the way that works best for them (Figure 6-2).

When the Integration No Longer Cuts It

It's time for a chatbot when the third-party integrations are:

- Not available
- Not flexible enough to work with your special "snowflake"
- Not feature rich or missing core functionality your team needs

---

Currently there are several well-known chatbots available, with more and more popping up all of the time. However, much of the media attention and conversations online about chatbots are more focused on the business-to-consumer (B2C) style of chatbot development.

Facebook and Twitter have been testing out a variety of chatbots from within their services, attempting to add more functionality and touchpoints for their users. Retail companies are also experimenting with bots that integrate with their ecommerce stores, allowing customers to interact from within chat. While this discussion around chatbots and the related development targeting social media and retail is interesting and gaining much attention, these are not the types of bots that we are referring to when we talk about ChatOps. Much can be learned and gained from understanding these bots and how they work, but for our purposes we are primarily focused on chatbots that help our teams manage their day-to-day work lives rather than facilitating interaction with consumers.

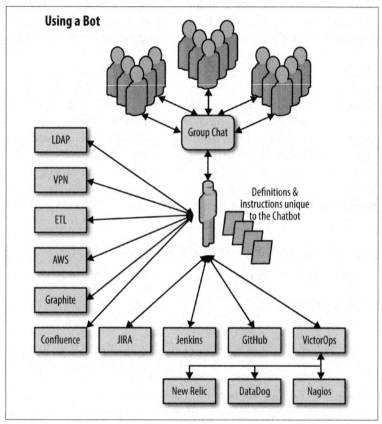

Figure 6-2. Using a chatbot

Hubot

The most well-known chatbot available today is Hubot (*https:// hubot.github.com/*). A Node.js application extensible with Coffee-Script or JavaScript, Hubot was originally developed by GitHub for internal use only. Later, GitHub rebuilt Hubot from the ground up and open-sourced the project, making it available to the public and allowing others to contribute to its ongoing development. Because it has been around the longest, the number of contributors to the core application as well as the growing list of scripts that manage the interactions with third-party services, the infrastructure, and the codebase is larger than for any other chatbot available today.

Lita

As ChatOps has gained in popularity, a chatbot written in Ruby named Lita (*https://www.lita.io/*) has caught the attention of teams around the world. Definition files and instructions are written in Ruby in the form of modules that allow much of the same functionality that Hubot provides. With a strong and growing community consistently contributing to the source code and modules, this chatbot has become very popular and easy to implement.

Errbot

Errbot (*http://errbot.io/*) is an open source project written in Python. It has a number advantages over both Lita and Hubot, the most notable one being that the application does not need to be restarted each time a new script is added to the library. Errbot is able to recognize new Python scripts and begin running them on behalf of users as soon as they have been placed in the correct directory. Following its nearly complete redesign a year ago, Errbot has a gentle learning curve and intriguing features to consider. These include:

- Ability to "pipe" commands, automation, and conversations
- Ability to manage the bot through chat
- Built in ACLs for security

Cog

Cog (*http://operable.io/*) is another new player in the ChatOps space, but it's much more than simply a bot. Cog is engineered to be more of a framework that addresses a number of concerns many teams have, such as security. With built-in access control and audit logging functionality, Cog allows teams to collaborate on sensitive tasks with higher confidence. Taking inspiration from the command-line interface, Cog has a "pipe" operator that allows users to run a command and use that output as the input for another command in a process.

Yetibot

Recently a new chatbot named Yetibot (*https://github.com/devth/yetibot*) has caught the attention of some. A self-proclaimed "communal command line," Yetibot is written in Clojure. This chatbot has a few features that may pique the interest of technical teams looking to piece together strings of commands. Similar to Cog's piping functionality, Yetibot allows users to chain together complex and flexible commands as well as letting you embed the output of one command into an outer command. Commands can be nested as many levels deep as you like.

Instructing Chatbots

When it comes to instructing your bot to take action on your behalf, the scripts, modules, or files that contain instructions will vary depending on your choice of bot. Hubot is a Node.js application and therefore requires instructions and definition files to be authored in either CoffeeScript or JavaScript. Ruby is the language of Lita, and for those who wish to instruct their bots using Python, Errbot may be where you start. Yetibot, of course, is instructed using Clojure files, and Cog is extensible in any language.

Bot and Language-Agnostic Libraries

Coming to a consensus on which bot and (as a result) programming language to use is often difficult, especially for larger organizations with many teams. There is another approach that enables leveraging the power of disparate services and bots. A strong argument can be made[1] that it is much better to build a library of automation scripts written in any language that can be accessed via not only a group chat tool, but also an API, command-line interface, or graphical user interface (see Figure 6-3). Because there are multiple ways to interact with a library of scripts, teams can focus more on building small, decoupled automation scripts that can be peer reviewed, version controlled, and made available across the organization. Fine-grained access control can be put in place to ensure those who should have the ability to execute commands can and those that shouldn't can't.

This adds a level of abstraction away from the complex inner workings of the automation scripts. Actions can be exposed to teams with complete disregard for the programming language or chatbot in use. Teams are less likely to become dependent on any particular bot or programming language and thus can focus more on building small yet powerful scripts in their languages of choice. Any chatbot mentioned in this text or any other that may surface and evolve in the future will be able to execute these scripts regardless of the language it's developed in.

---

1 And has been—see for example *https://stackstorm.com/2015/12/10/chatops_pitfalls_and_tips/*.

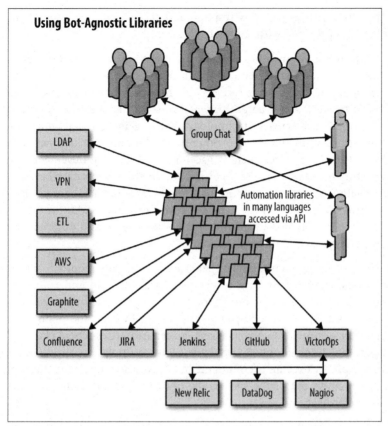

Using Bot-Agnostic Libraries

LDAP

VPN

ETL

AWS

Graphite

Group Chat

Automation libraries
in many languages
accessed via API

Confluence JIRA Jenkins GitHub VictorOps

New Relic DataDog Nagios

Figure 6-3. Using bot-agnostic automation libraries

Syntax: Command Versus Natural Language

One of the more interesting discussions surrounding chatbots and the future of their development is around the use of natural language versus command language. At present, all the chatbots we've looked at here require a very specific syntax in order to execute commands. Much like when inputting commands with variables, triggers, and flags from the command line, the bots will only execute your commands if they are typed or pasted into the chat client in a very specific way. Typing errors, missing variables, or an errant space will prevent the bot from executing anything. I'll touch on this more in Chapter 12, but the gist is that a basic layer of security is built into your interactions with the chatbots. Accidents are reduced because the bots will only respond and act on your behalf if a command is provided with complete accuracy.

With that said, some teams are experimenting with ways to create a more "human-like" interaction with their preferred chatbots. Natural language processing (NLP) and the development of associated APIs to allow more natural interactions with applications (such as chatbots) is an area of technology that is gaining more and more attention. With the surge in interest in chatbots that interact with social media services such as Facebook and Twitter, developers are seeking out ways to make the "back and forth" conversation between a chatbot and a human more natural. This requires enhanced algorithms that can take in many considerations. Additionally, it requires that that the algorithms are able to learn and optimize the experience over time for the end user.

Until operators familiarize themselves with the required syntax understood by their bots, interactions are less fluid and conversational. Also, context is not carried and disseminated throughout a conversation. However, by allowing the bot to store and maintain a history of previous conversations, a scenario arises where clarification on interactions is available. For example, if an operator attempts to execute a command but leaves an important piece of information out of the syntax, the bot can respond asking for further clarification.

Let's say I want to restart a service on a host. I may run a command such as:

```
>Jason  @bot restart apache
>bot:   I do not understand
```

In this example, I failed to pass along an important piece of information to the bot. I did not tell it which host or IP address I wanted to restart the *apache* service on. As result, the chatbot's only possible response was "I do not understand." If I engineer in logic so that the bot can ask a follow-up question, however, the interaction feels much more natural. An example of this would be:

```
>Jason:    @bot restart apache
>ChatBot:  @Jason on which host would you like to restart
           apache?
>Jason:    @bot 192.168.0.24
>ChatBot:  Restarting apache service on host 192.168.0.24
>ChatBot:  The apache service has been restarted
```

This allows for a much more pleasant and intuitive interaction, but a great deal of engineering is required to build in logic that can address the vast number of possible scenarios.

As ChatOps continues to evolve, the ability to use natural language processing with the chatbots to make the interactions more seamless and "human-like" will continue to improve. Operators will be able to interact with bots as though they are real-life members of the team. Through the use of natural language, users can begin carrying on conversations with bots rather than simply instructing them. Of course, this brings up the topic of artificial intelligence and what is likely to be the not-so-distant future of bots. We aren't quite there yet with regard to ChatOps, but the conditions are here to begin exploring ways to leverage NLP to open up even more functionality and benefits. Being able to immediately begin interacting with a chatbot, not knowing anything about the correct syntax, lowers the barrier to entry and provides exciting possibilities for what ChatOps may look like in the coming years.

CHAPTER 7

Getting Started and Examples

While evaluating and choosing the right tools for your situation is an important early step, you must first ask yourself and your team: "What is it we are trying to accomplish?" ChatOps was born out of DevOps principles. Because of that, teams must realize that it's important to use business objectives to prioritize efforts even with ChatOps.

TIP

Understand the "Why" of ChatOps

Before choosing a group chat tool, teams need to be informed of the "why" of ChatOps and its relationship to the company's objectives.

The idea of continuous improvement should always be in the minds of those trying to implement change—particularly when it comes to cultural change, which is what ChatOps represents. Increasing collaboration and sharing of information and knowledge is not a top-down initiative. It is something that must evolve over time. Tools and processes can be put in place to facilitate change, but it doesn't happen overnight.

There will be some within the team or organization who feel that a ChatOps effort is "just another project." They may not initially see it as creating a new and valuable way of managing the codebase, infrastructure, and more if business objectives are not made the clear priority. This situation is even worse if the capabilities and benefits of a ChatOps approach aren't made clear. Begin by understanding what is best for the company. Then communicate it clearly to the team and organization, and go from there.

Immediate benefits can and should be outlined to the team as you get started. In many cases, just the idea of reduced email interactions and pointless IM interruptions will be enough to win over those who are resistant to ChatOps.

Proof of Concept

It is often best to establish timelines to roll out a "proof of concept" for a number of chat clients and (if necessary) chatbots. I have mentioned a few of the popular tools and services available today, but by no means is this an exhaustive list. Each piece of technology has its strengths and weaknesses, and it's best to try a number of options before settling on one. Make it a team or organizational choice so that everyone feels invested in the direction things are moving in, or at the very least, make sure everyone's voices are heard.

Low-Hanging Fruit

Increased collaboration will naturally occur as teams move away from email and IM in favor of more synchronous conversations. Seek out tasks and processes that can be automated. Start where the changes will have the quickest or most immediate benefits. Tasks that address repetitive actions that can easily be automated are a great place to begin. Once those tasks have been reduced down to repeatable steps that can be assigned to a bot, move on to problems that are more challenging to address.

To figure out what to enable through ChatOps first, look for the "low-hanging fruit" of your work—that is, places where changes will be easiest to implement. By asking yourself a few questions, you can quickly come up with a list of things to tackle first.

Ask Yourself:

- What is something I commonly have to look up?
- What is a process that I do manually more than 3–5 times a day/week/month/year?
- What are questions people ask me frequently?
- What tasks do people often ask me to do for them?

Now, let's take a closer look at some of the more popular applications of ChatOps and possible good starting points for your team. Some of the examples outlined will require the use of a bot. Others are possible simply through the use of third-party plug-ins and your chosen chat client.

Without Chatbots

In Chapter 5, I pointed out that the types of interactions ChatOps is used for fall into a number of categories. There are push, pull, and bidirectional interactions. Pushing context is often where many teams begin their journeys, as it does not require the assistance of a chatbot. Rather, an integration of the service you are using with the chat tool of your choice handles the actions. Notifying teams or individuals of information that is relevant to them is the main goal here. At any given time, individuals may be interested in the status of a number of systems or activities. Rather than constantly checking on statuses manually, a simple integration with the service that is being used can allow for information, be it critical or informational, to be delivered to the appropriate person or teams in real time. These integrations are easy to set up and generally provide functionality that is simple yet helpful.

Repository Notifications

What better place to start with as an example than where the term ChatOps was born—GitHub? Many teams use this popular service to version-control and store their codebases. Throughout any given day, a lot of actions take place and information is made available on a variety of branches and projects. In many cases, engineers need to be made aware of those actions and changes quickly and effectively.

One way teams have found to ensure that relevant information is provided to them in the most efficient way is to notify engineers through group chat of activity in GitHub (see Figure 7-1).

Figure 7-1. GitHub notifications

By providing real-time context on activities throughout teams and departments, a greater awareness and understanding is reached. Less effort is needed to communicate critical information across an organization because the integration manages providing that information on your behalf.

Continuous Integration (CI) Notifications

Another popular use of third-party integrations for software and infrastructure engineers is to provide real-time "continuous integration" information regarding actions to build infrastructure. Each time code is checked into a repository, it is then verified by an automated build. This allows teams to identify and be notified of problems earlier in the development process. Tools and services such as Jenkins and Travis CI are used in cases like this (see Figure 7-2), and by allowing the integration to provide notifications to engineers, not only is relevant information shared beyond just those executing the actions, but the status updates are made available to everyone who needs to be aware of them in real time.

Figure 7-2. Travis notifications

Incident Management Notifications

Some notifications are nothing more than information that should be shared across teams. However, others are intended to alert individuals or teams to critical issues. Service disruptions and infrastructure outages are just part of the game when it comes to technology. Reducing the time it takes for the necessary people to be made aware of issues means a reduction in the time it takes to address and resolve problems. And when more people are made aware of situations and they are able to collaborate to investigate and solve those problems, services become much more stable and resilient. Thus, sending these types of alerts to a group chat provides a great deal of value to teams who are supporting and maintaining infrastructure and code.

Services like VictorOps provide actionable alerts directly to the right individuals and teams in a variety of ways, including via group chat (see Figure 7-3). When all timeline activity of the "on-call" team is in a shared chat environment, problems can be resolved in real time faster than ever. Because information about what is taking place during an incident is shared amongst a larger group, awareness increases and the "Time to Repair" (TTR) decreases.

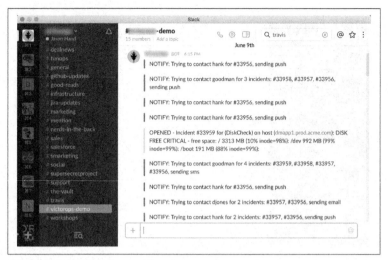

Figure 7-3. VictorOps notifications

Additional Third-Party Notification Examples

- New or updated support tickets
- Event or meeting reminders
- Planning and roadmapping activities
- Google Calendar notifications
- Security policy violations
- RSS feed changes
- Bug reports (created, closed, comments)

Call and Response

Many third-party integrations do have some sense of back and forth, but typically they are single round-trip interactions. For example, users can pass information along to Google to create a new Calendar event, and Google will echo a "success" response back to a group chat. Here are a few examples of this type of interaction:

- Language translations
- Establishing conference calls
- Creating Google Hangouts

- Creating Calendar events

By allowing the third party to do some of the work for us, we are free to focus our attention and efforts on other activities or responsibilities. Still, there are certain limitations with simple integrations. In most cases, they aren't interactive beyond a single call and response. Also, they may not provide all of the functionality we desire or even provide the answers to important questions that we need when we need them. This is where the need for chatbots becomes a reality.

Chatbots are much more flexible and powerful. Regardless of which bot you choose or whether you abstract all of the automation of your infrastructure and codebase through a library of scripts, the possibilities are boundless, and a chatbot can quickly become something resembling a very important member of your team—one that is always available and willing to do anything in its power for you.

With Chatbots

As you can see, there is some really great functionality that comes baked right into many third-party native integrations with persistent chat tools. However, limitations do exist, and teams may quickly discover that while the additional context that is provided in real time is helpful so long as it's not too noisy, there are bounds to its usefulness and flexibility. For some, the next logical step is to begin exploring the world of chatbots and the deeper functionality that can be provided through community-built scripts or ones engineered by the teams themselves. Once you have decided you are ready for a chatbot, a great place to start is by using or creating functionality to query information in a "read-only" manner. You can then move on as needed to the other CRUD (create, read, update, delete) operations.

Read

A multitude of information is obtainable through API calls to services teams use each and every day. By invoking calls to those services, information can be queried and presented back into the common chat environment. From there, operators can decide whether to act further. Additionally, a wealth of information may exist in local databases, logs, graphs, and more that are often difficult to query or view, depending on user access, privileges, or knowledge of how to obtain the data. By making this information more easily available and widely readable (and removing the dependency on others to unblock it), teams can become much more aware and cross-functional.

Examples

- Customer records in Salesforce
- Graphite or DataDog graphs
- Upcoming on-call schedule
- DNS records
- WHOIS database
- Incidents in VictorOps or PagerDuty

Create

Reading records is the most advisable place to start when first introducing a chatbot to your software and infrastructure management practices, but having the ability to trigger actions often means needing to create new records with the service you are interacting with. For example, you may need to create a new JIRA ticket or to-do list item following a postmortem and learning review. This can be accomplished right from the chat tool with the use of a chatbot and related instructions on how to interact with the service via an API. Team members will be able to *(c)*reate a record from chat (say, a JIRA ticket) quickly and easily, and others on the team will be able to see what was done and how. It's also timestamped, providing an accurate log and audit trail of what exactly was done and by whom.

- Create status pages
- Provision infrastructure
- Create new incidents in VictorOps or PagerDuty
- Create JIRA tickets
- Create to-do lists/items
- Submit new support tickets
- Alert on-call engineer(s)

Update

Almost as common as an activity creating a new record via a chatbot and script is the need to update existing records in a database or file. For instance, in order for an on-call engineer to acknowledge an alert when notified of a service disruption, a call needs to be made via an API to update a record on the service provider's endpoint.

- Acknowledge and resolve incidents in VictorOps or PagerDuty
- Update configuration files
- Update status pages
- Update Trello boards and to-do lists

Delete

It is not that common to find scripts to facilitate a simple record removal. In most cases, data is stored indefinitely, and rather than being removed from a datastore the record is changed to have an updated status (i.e., flagged as deleted). Nevertheless, as long as the API call to the service your bot is interacting with allows for record deletion, there is nothing inherently preventing you or your team from engineering a script for that sole purpose. One possible example of this type of action would be to "destroy" virtual or cloud infrastructure that is no longer needed.

Combination of CRUD Operations

For many teams, the full value of a chatbot is realized when several actions take place in one executed command. For example, a script might take an input from a user and *(u)*pdate a record, followed by retrieving information from a datastore about the next step to display back to the end user for a follow-up input. The user might then provide new information to *(c)*reate a new record, and so on.

> **NOTE**
>
> ### Examples
>
> - Two-factor authentication
> - Facilitating daily "stand-up" meetings
> - Group polling
> - Saving and retrieving bookmarks
> - Configuration management operations
> - Database migrations
> - Managing LDAP servers
> - Managing VPNs
> - Shortening URLs using Bitly or Google's URL shortener

CHAPTER 8

A World Connected by API

The underlying technology of ChatOps relies heavily on the use of application programming interfaces (APIs) to leverage the tools and services many of us use in our daily tasks. Over the last decade, APIs have become an integral part of both software development and infrastructure management. Services and tools that many in the software industry use commonly, such as GitHub, Jenkins, and VictorOps, provide API functionality to extend their usefulness beyond their original design. This, along with the efforts and spirit of the open source community, has allowed for further development and enhancements by teams across many disciplines.

A New Interface

Simple yet powerful APIs allow teams to build an abstraction layer as well as an entirely new user interface that better suits their or their organization's needs. Additionally, APIs allow distinct and disjointed applications to communicate and share information, further integrating and enhancing the overall functionality of the applications as a whole. Through the integration of separate systems via APIs, ecosystems are created that can help a business on a variety of levels. Disparate services that are commonly used independently can be tied together to work in orchestration. One example of this is the ability to automatically trigger infrastructure builds using a tool such as Jenkins when engineers commit new code to a version control repository service such as GitHub.

Within the context of ChatOps, we can interact with many services and tools via APIs and utilize a persistent group chat tool or service as the user interface. From within this collaborative environment, diverse operators are able to achieve their tasks, be they creating, reading, updating, or deleting (the CRUD operations mentioned in the previous chapter), from a common interface. In many cases the services behind the APIs can even interact with each other. When one service provides contextual information as output to the chat tool, another service can detect that output and take the desired additional steps.

 Just as the web browser has supplanted rich client interfaces, the group chat tool is now the interface of choice to view the work of others, accomplish your own tasks, and communicate those efforts at the same time with little to no extra effort.

Much of our work is visible from within a shared chat environment (see Figure 8-1). As a result, awareness is distributed evenly. Context about what is taking place provides real-time feedback to operators and stakeholders. Sharing actions, results, and documentation becomes an inherent part of the standard behavior. A user interacting with an API directly or via a chatbot can accomplish a vast and growing list of actions, with the added benefits of natural sharing, learning, and more.

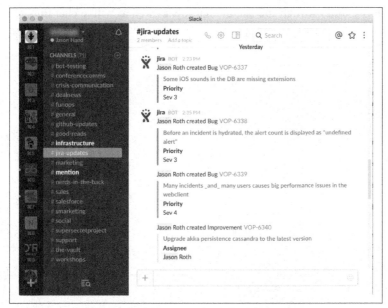

Figure 8-1. JIRA ticket information shared with the team

A Growing Ecosystem

Throughout every organization, teams have come to rely on many separate tools and services to accomplish their tasks. Some of those tools are proprietary systems that reside internally, in an organization's private network. Others are third-party services or offered by SaaS providers. Still others may simply be open source applications hosted either internally or externally, on a virtual machine or container, and are mostly immutable and portable. As mentioned in Chapter 7, many of these services provide CRUD functionality via an API. The result is that disparate systems that previously had no means of exchanging data or interacting with each other are suddenly part of a growing ecosystem and can be leveraged by more and more parts of the company.

If we look at current search trends (see Figure 8-2), we can see that interest in ChatOps has steadily increased in recent years. Following the explosive adoption of Slack, HipChat, and other group chat tools, teams have been able to leverage these services from an interface that already exists, is easy to understand, is familiar, and is not an additional piece of software that needs to be maintained and supported. More and more teams are turning to persistent group chat tools, and through the use of chatbots as well as native chat integrations, they are beginning to realize increases in not only sharing, but so much more.

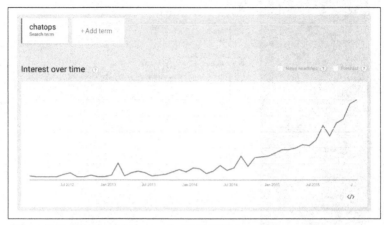

Figure 8-2. Google search trends 2012–2016

CHAPTER 9

Infrastructure as Conversation

Much of the evolution of ChatOps started with software engineers managing source code from the comfort of their chat clients. As outlined in Chapter 5, these are still some of the most common use cases. Originally dubbed "conversation-driven development" at GitHub, ChatOps has evolved well beyond the ability to keep teams up-to-date on information regarding source control repositories. A broad range of teams now manage a large and growing list of services and actions related to IT operations and more.

If you are at all familiar with the principles and disciplines that have evolved from DevOps, you've likely heard the phrase "Infrastructure as Code" (IaC). The term refers to the practice of engineers provisioning and managing infrastructure through the use of definition files written in languages such as Ruby, Python, Java, and others. With the widespread adoption of cloud computing and remote data center usage, more and more teams and organizations are turning to IaC for managing these processes.

Traditional "Ops" teams are now engineering scripts written in programming languages that have historically only been used by software engineers. Configuration management services such as Chef, Puppet, Ansible, and SaltStack allow provisioning and management of infrastructure through scripts, triggers, and event actions.

As teams begin to adopt DevOps principles and share more of the roles and responsibilities, sharing becomes one of the key points of focus. Group chat is where most of this sharing takes place, both intentionally and inherently. Conversations about the development of software as well as infrastructure begin to unfold naturally in a space where everyone is part of the conversation. Thus, the creation, configuration, and support of infrastructure are managed from within a group chat interface.

Managing Infrastructure as a Collaborative Process

Today, teams are managing the development of code, its transit to a repository, and the ensuing notifications about what is taking place with that code. They are also building infrastructure using tools that allow for builds to be automatically triggered through commits to repositories, by scheduling, or based on the results of other actions. All of this is kicked off and managed from within group chat. And all of it is surrounded by conversations that are related to those actions, making the entire process much more collaborative.

Managing infrastructure as conversation brings the benefits of IaC along with the context and collaboration that is happening within group chat. The result is that more members of the team and the organization are aware of what is taking place in real time. They have the ability to learn from others how things get done, and can see what questions may come up during those actions and what countermeasures need to be initiated if something doesn't execute or behave as expected. The conversation about infrastructure provides an image of higher fidelity for not only those who are involved in the actions but also those who aren't, both as it is taking place and for review later.

Empowering Engineers

With the gain in DevOps adoption, many teams are beginning to dissolve the segregated responsibilities and roles that were traditionally divided up between "developers," "operations," and others. Now, those roles aren't so isolated and pragmatically separated. Teams are beginning to understand more about what takes place outside of their roles. Those who were historically specifically software engineers now have a better understanding of the infrastructure on which their software runs. As a result, they are more vested in making sure that the code they write and the infrastructure it will run on in a production environment are designed and maintained correctly.

Developers now understand more about infrastructure than ever before and are empowered to provision, configure, manage, and even terminate servers.

This shared understanding by both groups means that developers and operations teams are now more capable and therefore responsible for much more than ever before. A deeper understanding of the codebase and the infrastructure on which it runs makes way for a more reliable and feature-rich service or tool.

CHAPTER 10

The Convergence of Conversation, Context, and Action

As teams begin to move much more of their daily work into group chat, a convergence takes shape. Not only are team members able to gain insight into what is going on in other areas of the department or organization (whether they absolutely need to or not), but they are sharing more about their own actions and conversations for others to add to their ongoing and shifting snapshots of the situation. This increased awareness helps make the pulse of daily actions available to everyone.

It's not uncommon for organizations to use a chat tool for quick messages to team members, on topics that don't warrant the time and effort required for correspondence via email. In most cases, these conversations are unintentionally, yet actively, isolated from the rest of the team. Collaboration over a topic is difficult or impossible, simply because the tool in use or the culture of the teams and organizations in question do not facilitate it.

More Informed, Responsive, and Efficient

Chat applications and services have been around for quite some time, and teams within many organizations use them and, in some cases, chatbots to take tedious and repetitive tasks off of their plates. In many cases, a question such as "When am I on call next?" can be asked and responded to through a bot and API interaction in a fraction of the time it takes an operator to track down the information.

Serious work that requires more attention and cognitive load can then be given the time it requires, allowing teams to focus on and put more effort into learning, improving, and innovating.

Many of the ideas and principles that are labeled as "ChatOps" have been around for quite some time. The standard protocol known as Internet Relay Chat (IRC) has been leveraged since 1988 and is still being used today by companies for their own internal group communication. Although private conversations are still popular amongst users of IRC and modern persistent group chat tools, the group "rooms" or "channels" are where most conversations take place.

Real-Time Awareness

There's a good reason for this. The conversations, related context, and actions taken by team members are all captured in real time for everyone to see. By pulling all of this information about what is taking place and how, along with the results, into a single interface, teams are able to realize multiple levels of benefits. Because everything is captured in one place, institutional knowledge is disseminated across the team. A greater awareness is provided to all who are part of the chat room. Actions and conversations are logged, creating a real-time log of what took place while also detailing critical information needed for postmortems, retrospectives, or learning reviews.

When teams begin to take actions and move all of the related context to within a shared interface, organizations begin to see real traction and velocity in their efforts to become highly effective and cross-functional. It's through this convergence that more and more are able to get a pulse on what is taking place outside of their own responsibilities. And it's through this behavior that we begin to see those artificially isolated conversations begin to move back into a common space where a larger number of people can not only take part, but also synchronize their awareness on exactly what is taking place, how it was accomplished, and what the result is.

CHAPTER 11

Make Work Visible

ChatOps helps to combine and facilitate key principles of not only DevOps, but Agile and Lean methodologies as well. By removing friction and waste in our processes as well as making the actions (automated or not) visible to more of the team from within group chat, a clearer picture begins to emerge. Teams have access to a record of not only how things get done, but the conversations that are related to those actions.

Many teams have realized that much of their daily repetitive work can be automated. Automation is one of the key principles of DevOps. By automating as much menial and repetitive work as possible, teams and organizations are able to free up more time to focus on new or harder tasks that cannot be automated just yet. Additionally, opportunities for exploration, experimentation, and innovation are made available when teams and their members aren't spending unnecessary time duplicating efforts. By making that automation and the related conversations visible to more people, a number of benefits emerge.

Benefits of Making Work Visible

- Create common frame of reference
- Expose friction and bottlenecks in processes
- See pain points together (i.e., create empathy)
- Reduce work in progress
- Swarm to problems together
- Generate multiple perspectives
- Document work in real time
- Uncover areas of improvement
- Create greater awareness for all

It's likely that you or members of your team have already begun to automate much of your work, especially in the context of information technology. There are many tools on the market today that help teams automate specific portions of their work. Typically the automation is executed manually, but it's not unlikely that some of it is achieved completely autonomously through the use of schedulers, scripts, and triggers. This time-saving behavior is not a new approach to work, but it is evolving.

Leverage a Bot

Through the efforts of a ChatOps approach, teams are able to take automation even further. With the right setup and configuration, existing automation that may have already been in place can now be executed and made visible from within a persistent group chat tool. For example, teams that are using "continuous delivery" practices can configure a bot not only to assist in the committing of code to a version control repository but to trigger the building of virtual infrastructure when a new code commit has taken place, thereby providing the ability to automate several steps that previously required an operator to execute manually, wait for results, and then proceed with the next steps in the process. Legacy automation can be made available for authorized users right from within the same location where teams are discussing topics relevant or related to the automation and its results.

We're now able to take the actual actions or specific syntax necessary to complete a task and trigger it from within an interface where everyone in the team is active and where everyone can stay informed. The results of those actions are instantly made available to the rest of the team (or organization), without any need for further action from the operator running the command. Feedback on what took place, how it was accomplished, and the result is clear and immediate. Even better, it's available to all who are interested.

Through increased visibility into what is taking place and how, and the outcome, more awareness is created. Information on how to accomplish a task is removed from any possible single point of failure with regard to people, and it's all documented. Exactly who did what and when is placed directly inline with the conversations related to those actions.

Remote Work Force

Not all organizations have distributed or remote workers, but for those that do, ChatOps allows teams to share the same context, awareness, and capabilities equally, regardless of any individual's physical location and time zone.

Greater awareness of the status of systems and the actions being taken by other members of the team helps spread the load as well. This creates a scenario where operators within and across multiple teams can not only gain a deeper understanding of subjects beyond their core expertise, but also begin to gain a sense of empathy for those with different responsibilities. As a result, more and more members of the team or organization can come to understand how to accomplish a task and what the expected results should be, and will then be able to assist (whether by having access to additional context or knowing exactly what needs to be done under specific circumstances).

Once teams have a deeper understanding of the automation that is used within their own infrastructure, codebase, projects, and more, areas of improvement will be uncovered. It's amazing to see members of a team seek out new actions to automate, further removing bottlenecks and freeing up their own time to tackle harder puzzles or more cognitively challenging tasks.

Spread Tribal Knowledge

A common trait of highly effective, cross-functional teams is the ability to collaborate, sharing conversations, information, and actions. Being able to do so quickly, easily, and in a way that feels familiar and natural helps with adoption and leads to sharing more of what takes place within teams and the organization as a whole. As individuals move more about what they are thinking, saying, seeing, and doing into a common space for more members of the team to see, an interesting thing begins to take place: tribal knowledge on a growing number of topics is spread beyond just a handful of individuals.

As this knowledge spreads, more and more people become aware of what is taking place throughout the workday in areas of the organization that they typically had little to no insight into. Admittedly, this isn't always necessary or even desired. However, the awareness brought to more of the team and management simply by abandoning email and instant messaging (IM) in favor of persistent group chat for all internal conversations is what sets these highly effective teams apart from the rest.

Familiar and Predictable

By moving conversations, actions, and context into an interface that is familiar and predictable, standardization in how teams communicate and collaborate in real time begins to take shape. Through this real-time collaborative interface, many teams have realized that much of their daily repetitive work can not only be automated but also executed and contextualized in a single familiar place: group chat.

Building Empathy

Encouraging empathy between teams that are often at odds with each other is at the heart of DevOps. Conflicting departmental or individual goals and key performance indicators (KPIs) in many cases cause unnecessary friction internally. Because isolated teams have little to no knowledge of what takes place outside of their own roles and responsibilities, it's nearly impossible for everyone to be on the same page with regard to the overall success of a project or even the business as a whole. Instead, they focus solely on the tasks, deadlines, and goals assigned to them with no regard for what is going on elsewhere. The "it's not my problem" mentality then begins to become very prevalent throughout the company. Once that has happened, any chance of becoming a highly effective team starts to break down.

Later, I'll discuss the importance of having captured snapshots of the time at which something took place. Issues such as compliance and tasks like post-incident analysis rely heavily on having accurate timelines of actions and conversations that document in real time exactly what took place (see Figure 11-1). Automation plays a big role in the modern business world. Making it visible in real time as well as capturing it for review later is a great way to create empathy, uncover areas for improvement, and provide the necessary documentation to those who need it.

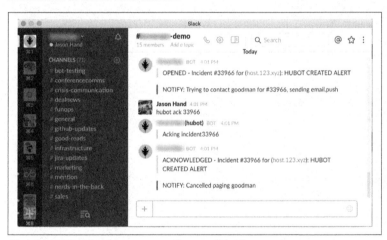

Figure 11-1. Capturing actions for post-incident review

CHAPTER 12

Security and Safety

Before I discuss the benefits, challenges, and concerns regarding security as it relates to ChatOps, I must point out that I'm not an expert in this field. Cybersecurity and system safety compliance are broad and dense topics far beyond the scope of this text. The specific concerns will of course vary from organization to organization, and you should make time for careful consideration and discussion as you begin to roll out your own ChatOps initiative.

With that said, one of the many benefits of ChatOps is that, to a certain degree, a soft layer of security is built in. Even the most powerful custom actions that leverage a chatbot to execute commands, query information, and more have restrictions hardcoded into the instructions and definitions. When a user attempts to execute a command using the incorrect syntax, the chatbot will inform the user that it does not understand what it's being asked to do. It will only execute commands that are part of its coded instructions. In the event that the user makes a mistake when inputting a command, the same result will happen. Conversely, if a user were to execute syntax from a command line and make a mistake, there could be a negative outcome, and perhaps not something that can be recovered from. Use of the command line combined with high-level access to a system can lead to disaster when mistakes are made.

Security Through Obscurity

ChatOps creates an abstraction layer for end users to interact with systems in a safe way while also teaching others how it's done. It's a way for us to query and navigate sensitive data, build infrastructure, and more without the need to request access to systems we may not fully understand. Still, security is a much larger topic than simply the concern of fat-fingering a command.

There are many security and safety concerns to consider as you begin implementing ChatOps internally.

Ask Yourself:

- How do we authorize a user to execute a sensitive command?

- How do we prevent provisioning of unnecessary and expensive infrastructure?

- How do we ensure untrained individuals aren't able to cause service disruptions accidentally?

- How do we protect intellectual property (IP) that resides on a hosted provider's infrastructure?

- What if the hosted chat service is temporarily unavailable? How do we get work done?

For some—especially larger organizations that have strict security policies and a growing list of compliance concerns to deal with—this is the deal-breaker of ChatOps. In some cases, the discussion of even using a modern persistent group chat tool is where the conversation starts and stops. The idea of storing sensitive company data on servers not owned by the corporation goes against company policy. The only option for these organizations is an "on-premise" chat solution. However, that means additional work supporting and maintaining that internal chat service, which means additional efforts and costs that must be considered.

But what about those who have decided that moving data to the cloud really is safe and the direction that the company is headed in? What happens if the service provider is compromised? It's happened before and is likely to happen again. What concerns are there for a company in that situation? Obviously, the attack surface becomes much larger if that information reaches individuals or groups with malicious intent, but what else do they need to think about?

Community to the Rescue

Presently, there are many within the ChatOps community who are discussing and engineering ways to address security concerns.[1] Although many of the existing and widely used chatbots available are open source, contributors to those projects are beginning to add components that allow for interaction with authorization services or internally hosted Lightweight Directory Access Protocol (LDAP) or Active Directory (AD) servers. By establishing user-, group-, and role-based rules regarding who can execute commands, many of the existing security concerns of organizations can be addressed.

As mentioned previously, all commands are automatically captured in real time from within the chat client, including details of who executed the commands and timestamps. Additionally, a few chatbots and ChatOps frameworks currently under development (such as Cog) are providing access control functionality and logging for audit and reporting purposes. This further addresses the compliance control and safety concerns that prohibit many organizations from exploring the opportunities and benefits that ChatOps may provide them.

Security Tip

Two-factor authentication (2FA) is one method teams have implemented to provide stricter security with ChatOps.

Leveraging a tool or service such as Google's Authenticator means users can confirm an action and ensure that the executed command has been authenticated properly.

---

1 See, for example, Michael Ansel's blog post "Securing ChatOps to Enable DevOps" (*https://www.box.com/blog/securing-chatops-enable-devops/*).

CHAPTER 13

Importance of Persistent Data

One of the important aspects of ChatOps is that the conversations, context, and commands executed are stored indefinitely. Because the data is persistent, topic-based discussions not only evolve over time but are easily searchable and retrievable from any point in the future. Because of this, participants of topic-based rooms or channels can review the chat and command history at any time, allowing them to easily get up to speed on recent or historic conversations and actions and their context. Individuals who join the conversations later can quickly get to the same level of awareness as those who participated in the conversations as they happened.

Topic-based discussions are easily separated by containing specific types of content to their own unique rooms or channels. This means that conversations, context, and actions regarding a service disruption, for example, can and should take place only within the room or channel that is associated with that topic. This helps to create a sterile space for collaboration that is dedicated solely to that topic. As the topics evolve over time, these unique yet specific spaces for conversations provide an ideal location for team members to share ideas, concepts, thoughts about improving processes and tooling, and more.

Unlike with email and instant messaging, the conversations in group chat are always available and searchable, and you can even create rules so you are alerted only about specific topics or actions you care about and aren't distracted constantly by things that aren't relevant to your work.

Let's take a look at a few examples of how persistent data from group chat can help to facilitate more than just the ChatOps efforts of your team.

Logs

Previously, I've mentioned the importance of security. Some aspects of the security concerns and conversations are tied to our efforts with logging. Logs provide a wealth of information both in real time and after the fact, when we need reliable data with accurate time-stamps to make sense of something. Because the data contained in group chat (including conversations, context, and commands) is persistent, logging practices are effortless and ongoing. When the logs from a snapshot in time are required to understand something, there is great comfort in knowing that the data is stored safely and is easily available.

Compliance

Closely related to logging, compliance control is another area where persistent data can help teams and organizations. Auditors will need to review logs in order to ensure policies and procedures are being adhered to. Because in group chat, conversations, actions, and their context are captured in real time and stored indefinitely, teams are able to address any compliance concerns that are brought to them.

Wikis

Wikis are a great way to capture important company information and make it easily available to everyone. Anyone who is tasked with authoring a wiki article on a specific topic will be pleased to find that much of the content they need is already stored in the persistent group chat. They can simply synthesize the content and organize it in a way that is easy for others to understand.

Onboarding

Some companies who have fully adopted ChatOps use persistent group chat and the associated data as the primary method for onboarding new employees. Because so much great detail about what goes on within teams and organizations is stored in group chat, it's very easy for new employees to join the rooms or channels that are associated with their roles and responsibilities to quickly get up to speed on "how things work around here."

Postmortems, Retrospectives, and Learning Reviews

Service disruptions are unavoidable. The complex IT systems and services that we engineer and support for internal and external users are going to have problems. The easiest way to improve these services and make them more reliable and available is to constantly and consistently learn from failures and outages. Because of this, postmortems (like the one in Figure 13-1) are essential to every IT team and organization.

Figure 13-1. Sample postmortem report/learning review

Group chat can provide extremely valuable information for these reports, from the initial alerting of a problem to what took place throughout the investigation, triaging, and remediation. This generates a very useful story, providing a record not only of the raw data that was created during the incident, but also the conversations that operators were having while trying to restore service. When these back-and-forth conversations are placed in line with the additional context from graphs or logs and the commands that team members were executing, you have a very accurate snapshot of what took

place during recovery efforts. Using that data, teams can then iden‐
tify areas for incremental improvement. Without the persistent stor‐
age of that data, building a postmortem would rely mostly on the
memory of those who were involved.

CHAPTER 14

Signal Versus Noise

It's important to note and discuss one common complaint about a ChatOps approach: the potential overload of conversations and alerts (i.e., *noise*). In smaller teams and organizations, the volume of conversations, context, and commands that flows through a group chat tool may seem manageable. As those teams grow, however, it becomes much harder to find ways to take part in the conversations, maintain awareness of what is taking place, and actually get your job done. When chat rooms or channels are constantly updating with new bits of information to ingest and process, it can actually become more detrimental to productivity than it is helpful.

Alert Fatigue

Alert fatigue is a very real concern that should be addressed as quickly as it's recognized. A failure to properly deal with alert fatigue can lead to not only a drop in productivity, but something much worse—burnout. The result of many contributing factors, burnout must be taken seriously and addressed immediately.

▼! Alert Fatigue

Exposure to a high volume of frequent alerts, causing desensitization to critical issues and leading to:

- Longer response times
- Anxiety
- Sleep deprivation
- Negative physical effects
- Employee dissatisfaction

Those who feel overwhelmed by their roles and responsibilities may not even realize that they are nearing a burnout situation. Alert fatigue is one of the contributing factors. At the end of the day it's up to each individual team member to decide how, how often, and on what topics they should be alerted. If a conversation is taking place regarding something that is specifically relevant to them and actionable, they will likely want to be notified about it. For conversations that do not meet those criteria, team members should be able to decide on their own whether to take part and if it's important for them to understand the context related to those conversations and to know how to execute the relevant commands should the need ever arise.

Make Adjustments

Finding the right signal-to-noise ratio is an ongoing effort. Adjusting alert settings, abandoning channels and rooms that you don't need to constantly monitor, and even temporarily shutting down the group chat tool entirely are all acceptable ways to manage that ratio. Group chat tools, chatbots, and anything else that has evolved out of the ChatOps conversation is designed to make life (and work) easier and more efficient. It provides several benefits that are hard to ignore. However, if someone on your team begins to feel overwhelmed by the onslaught of information, the reverse effect begins to set in.

Tips for Avoiding Alert Fatigue

- Make all alerts actionable.
- Reduce redundant alerts.
- Isolate alerts to appropriate rooms/channels.
- Adjust integration and anomaly detection thresholds.
- Ensure the right people or teams are alerted.
- Customize personal notifications.
- Regularly revisit all of the above for continuous improvements.

Set the Tone

For teams and organizations that are made up of hundreds or thousands of people, many in different time zones all around the world, the idea of even a small percentage of those people carrying on conversations, querying information, and running commands from within group chat may be enough to cause reconsideration of the wiseness of rolling out a ChatOps initiative. The most important thing to remember is to start small. Over time, more and more will join in the conversations. They will engineer new ways to interact with the services and tools used each day. They will find ways to keep the topics of discussion specific and on point. Casual conversations should take place in a different, more appropriate channel, and that self-imposed "rule of group chat" will start to take hold. In most cases, teams will curate conversations and encourage adherence to these concepts themselves, but for larger organizations it may be necessary for upper management to communicate with the teams and set the tone on how to properly manage conversations within the proper channels or rooms.

Continuous Improvement

Continuously assessing and improving the conversations, context, and commands used within group chat should always be made a priority.

Continuous improvement is what DevOps has brought to the conversation about IT operations and beyond. There is no concept of "done." It's an iterative process, and one that demands constant analysis in retrospect to identify areas for new and incremental improvements. ChatOps is no different. Chat clients will continue to evolve and become more useful and powerful. Chatbots are quickly iterating and improving. New programming languages and frameworks are popping up all of the time. It's part of the natural process of innovation in technology, and you are part of that.

Group chat is now a common interface for many things. Conversations about projects, issues, and planning take place there. Valuable insights and alerts are available there. Chatbots that listen for our commands and execute them on our behalf are always available and eager to serve. Third-party integrations to a growing list of services, all fighting for our attention, can be plugged into chat in mere seconds. In time, it will be possible for nearly every task in our daily routines to be managed from group chat. Along with those interactions will be conversations and added information that we didn't know we needed until it was placed in front of us. As a result, there will be a lot to deal with. Proper pruning and improving of the experience is absolutely necessary and should be made a high priority from the very beginning.

Pruning and Improving Suggestions

- Create topic-specific channels or rooms.
- Establish "sterile room" guidelines to stay on topic.
- Assess third-party integrations regularly to review usefulness.
- Regularly review channels or rooms subscribed to and remove unnecessary noise.

CHAPTER 15

Reliance on Third-Party Chat Service

In Chapter 12 we discussed some of the concerns of ChatOps regarding security. In many cases, organizations are not able to utilize SaaS offerings due to company policy. On-premise installations of any and all services leveraged by the company's end users are absolutely required to fall in line with security policies. Not being in control of company data or intellectual property are concerns that keep security officers up at night, and for good reason. There are other concerns with using a "hosted" service as well.

The software and infrastructure on which all SaaS offerings operate is extremely complex. As a result, occasional failure or disruption of services is unavoidable. At some point, the hosted service that your team or organization relies on is going to have some sort of minor (or major) outage that impacts your ability to get work done. We all hope that the entity hosting and managing the service will be able to detect it, alert us, and repair the problem as quickly as possible, but some times outages last far longer than hoped. How does that impact your team and organization? In some cases it could mean little more than an extended coffee break until the status page of the service gives the "service restored" update. In other cases it may mean a loss of income. The possible ramifications are varied and abundant.

Because of this, many companies are hesitant to rely on third-party services. In the event that something very bad happens to a SaaS provider that they rely on, it can have a huge impact on their own business. In the not-so-distant past, an outage to a group chat provider may not have caused much harm. However, for teams that now rely on ChatOps as part of their software delivery pipeline, for maintenance of infrastructure, and more, any kind of outage experienced by the provider could have a large impact.

Much of this speaks to the larger question of "hosted vs. on-prem." Again, in some cases company policy requires that all services and tools used by the organization reside on the company's private network and are managed either by the IT team or as part of a service agreement from the software provider. Until leadership within the organization has taken the time to truly understand the full picture of both scenarios, there may be little that can be done if you are hoping to roll out a group chat tool that is purely SaaS.

Run It On-Premise

There are options for those that find themselves unable to rely on a third-party service provider for chat. A few of the group chat tools offer an "on-prem" solution. I've also discussed how some teams are using IRC as their group chat tool. While it's not nearly as slick and user-friendly, there are many large and well-known companies using IRC internally to manage their ChatOps efforts with great success. Adoption of ChatOps beyond the technical teams could be a challenge, but it may offer a good starting point.

Going with an open source chat tool may be a good path to take in these situations as well. IT teams will still have to install, manage, and support the software, but hosting all of the data internally will ease the concerns of many who push back against relying on a hosted provider.

Once the organization has done its due diligence on whether or not it makes sense to build, support, and improve a large, complex system, you may be able to look at a hosted solution. When deciding which way to go, there are several questions to consider.

NOTE **Hosted Versus On-Prem**

- Does company policy prohibit the use of hosted service providers?

- Do you have the resources to install and configure an on-prem solution?

- Do you have the resources to support an on-prem solution, including upgrades, security patches, and remediating service disruptions?

- Will building, maintaining, and improving your own internal chat solution bring value to the business?

- Do you have the budget to absorb the associated costs?

If you answered "no" to most of the above considerations, your best option is a hosted group chat provider. Discussion of these items should involve the whole team or organization, so that all stakeholders understand why the decision to use a hosted provider was made.

Single Point of Failure

The main thing to remember is that regardless of whether you choose to use a hosted group chat service or host your own internal group chat, outages will occur. Teams should be able to fall back to alternative methods of managing code repositories, infrastructure changes, incidents, and more. ChatOps is a way of making our work easier and it provides a slew of benefits, but it relies on a chat client to be operational. In the event that chat is not available, teams will have to change course temporarily and manage their work in a more traditional manner. Preparation for the unavoidable situation of your chat service or chatbot being unavailable for an extended amount of time should be something all teams consider. ChatOps may be the "new" way of getting things done, but similar to a department store whose point of sale (POS) system becomes temporarily unavailable, there must be an alternative way of accomplishing all critical tasks. While it's not as efficient or nice an experience, just as a retail check-out clerk may have to use a carbon copy machine to process a credit card transaction, your team should have an alternate way of deploying code, acknowledging incidents, or completing any other process that has been moved to a ChatOps method.

Manual Labor

When we first began our own ChatOps journey at VictorOps, one of the first things I wanted to simplify and automate was the process of extending trials for new users. By default, all new users receive 14 days for free. However, two weeks isn't always enough to properly trial a service.

Myself or someone from our customer support team would regularly field requests to extend trials. Because a change like this would be made on a production database, we would then request assistance from an engineer to safely make the change. We did this a lot, and over time it became distracting and annoying to our developers.

A simple script was developed that would allow an authorized user (created specifically for this role) to execute a SQL UPDATE command and change the expiration date field in the database. This script was then made executable from within our group chat tool via Hubot.

Any time someone requested a trial extension, myself or someone from our support team could then run a simple command from within Slack and report back quickly to the user that their trial had been extended. Getting feedback to a potential customer that quickly goes a long way toward earning their business.

These days, that process has been improved even further to provide better assurances that authorized users are the only ones able to execute the trial extension. This helps to enable more of our team to take action in a secure way.

Most importantly, someone can always execute the commands manually from the command line. Even when Slack is dealing with a service disruption, we can still accomplish what we need to get done simply by doing it an alternate, manual way.

CHAPTER 16

Selling ChatOps to Your Boss

In Chapter 14, I discussed the importance of managing the signal-to-noise ratio. A busy chat room can become more of a liability than an asset if the conversations, alerts, etc. become too much to keep up with. For larger organizations the sheer number of team members participating in conversations, pulling in additional information, or executing commands can quickly become overwhelming. On top of that, enterprise organizations have concerns and priorities that are often different from those of small businesses or startups. Policies, procedures, and bureaucratic behaviors often stifle the benefits that something like ChatOps can bring to the table.

Despite these concerns, ChatOps is an extremely powerful and effective way of getting work done. Finding the right language to use with leadership is important in order to successfully begin your ChatOps journey.

Redesigning IT's Role and Purpose

Highly effective teams led by managers who understand the requirement of continuous change will likely embrace the idea of ChatOps. Today's CIOs realize that their most important role is to lead IT teams to redesign their own purpose. IT is no longer there to simply maintain and support systems for other departments in the company. IT is now the primary influencer in continuously improving processes and tools on behalf of users, both internal and external. The modern IT leader enables adaptation to change, recognizing the importance of continuous incremental improvements and treating the journey as the destination. The focus is on minimizing friction and latency in systems in order to create more effective feedback loops.

Group chat and bots, plug-ins, and third-party integrations are what provide that feedback loop in a lot of ways. Teams have much higher fidelity into the big picture of their systems and processes. They are able to be made aware of situations faster than ever and react in real time to the always-changing conditions.

Exposing Conversations and Collaboration

Nearly every large organization today has some sort of internal chat tool that is used to communicate. However, in many cases, these tools are not persistent and they do not allow for group conversations. They are typically designed more for one-on-one text, audio, or video interactions to facilitate closed discussions. The problem with these kinds of interaction is that the conversation is isolated from the rest of the team. Any important information that is shared or discussed in a private chat, audio, or video conversation does not make it to a wider audience. Granted, sometimes private conversations are necessary, but by and large open and transparent discussions amongst entire teams provide far greater benefits.

> **TIP**
> Sharing is a key component of DevOps. Transparency, building tribal knowledge, and gaining a greater awareness are what lead to high-performing, cross-functional teams. Isolating conversations to just a few parties prevents the level of sharing that is necessary in order to be effective and efficient.

An early step large enterprise organizations should take is to adopt a tool that allows for large groups to collaborate and engage in conversations in specific rooms or channels that are unique to the topic at hand. This does not have to be rolled out to the entire organization all at once. In fact, it may prove to be more effective and easier to implement by starting with smaller groups and over time bringing more and more teams and departments into the fold. Starting a new group chat initiative with hundreds or thousands of users all at once may turn out to be an exercise in chaos and hinder your efforts to implement ChatOps throughout the organization. Allow the technical teams to ease into including context with the conversations.

Establish soft policies on what types of executions can be run from within the chat client.

CHAPTER 17

Beyond the Horizon: The Future of ChatOps

I hope that you have found this text to be informative and helpful in your efforts to understand ChatOps and what it can bring to your team or organization. IT departments are now sources of innovation not only for their own efforts, but for the company as a whole. CIOs and the teams that they manage are now tasked with much more than just keeping the lights on and putting out fires as they occur. They are the innovators, always seeking out methods to reduce friction in the ways they deliver software, manage infrastructure, and provide a reliable service to end users, be that internally or externally.

ChatOps brings a new methodology to the table that many are finding great value in. Speeding up the way we get work done and delivering many additional benefits without any extra effort is something that can spark real organizational change—change that can lead to big ideas and innovations that set an organization apart from others in its market. DevOps has helped shed light on basic concepts that have been lost over the years: simple ideas such as empathy, open communication, aligned goals, and continuous improvement.

As ChatOps continues to evolve and mature, where will it go? Of course, it's all speculative at this point, but I believe it's fair to say that getting work done in chat is here to stay. With the surge of chatbots recently and their effortless interaction with a growing list of tools and services, more and more who are part of this movement are finding really interesting ways of dealing with the tasks and challenges that they face each day. Solving complex problems in creative and innovative ways is what software and infrastructure engineers dream about. ChatOps provides the space for them to realize new possibilities, whether that is by designing and building the next great persistent group chat tool, an extensible chatbot, or powerful APIs.

Advancements in Technology

When it comes to ChatOps, I believe we will continue to see great advancements in all areas. Chat clients are becoming more powerful, flexible, and user-friendly with each new version release. Chatbots are beginning to take on more and more tasks that can and should be automated, allowing engineers to focus their efforts on more complex tasks and puzzles. Natural language processors and the algorithms behind them are moving us closer to being able to interact with chatbots and the services that they interact with in ways that seem like talking to another person.

As this evolution takes place, new concerns will arise. Security will continue to be a concern as the technology matures and innovations emerge. Companies will face new challenges and opportunities. Continuously improving the way we get tasks done will start to become the major focus of not only IT teams, but entire organizations. With that focus, paths will unfold that aren't possible yet today.

Final Thoughts

ChatOps is a new way for us to get work done, particularly within the context of software and IT operations management. DevOps has brought forth many discussions about automation, sharing, removing friction, and more. ChatOps is an extension of those concepts. Finding new ways to do old tasks in order to enable more of the team, create a broader and more accurate awareness, and speed up tasks is at the heart of DevOps. ChatOps is one way teams have begun exploring those ideas, and it's exciting to see the innovation that has come about in only a handful of years.

As with any significant change in the way we think about and approach the work we do, it will take some time for your team or organization to fully realize the benefits that can be gained through a ChatOps approach. Throughout this report, I've outlined steps to consider as you begin. However, there is no truly prescriptive approach to ChatOps. Because so much of it requires a cultural change within your team or organization, your efforts and experiences will vary from everyone else's. Nevertheless, it's nice to have a handy step-by-step guide to use as starting point. Below, you'll find a synopsis of all of those considerations and steps to get you started today.

10 Ways to Get Started Today

1. Discuss and align the goals of your ChatOps initiative.

2. Implement proof of concept exercises for group chat tools if you aren't already using one.

3. Commit to a group chat tool.

4. Browse the third-party marketplace for services your team uses regularly and integrate them into the appropriate rooms or channels.

5. Analyze your signal-to-noise ratio (i.e., actionable vs. non-actionable alerts and context) and adjust accordingly.

6. Identify which third-party integrations are *not* providing sufficient functionality or context.

7. Implement proof of concept exercises for chatbots, including existing scripts from the community.

8. Commit to a chatbot and discuss where the bot should be hosted.

9. Extend the functionality of your chatbot by engineering automation of repetitive or time-consuming tasks (note: start with the low-hanging fruit).

10. Continuously review integrations and chatbot functionality for improvements.

I wish you good luck in your efforts to bring ChatOps to your team or organization, and I hope to find out one day that this report played a role in generating ideas and motivation to help you realize your own improvements!

About the Author

Jason Hand is a DevOps Evangelist at VictorOps, organizer of DevOpsDays–Rockies, author of *ChatOps for Dummies* (Wiley), and cohost of the "Community Pulse" podcast about building community in tech. He has spent the last 18 months presenting and building content on a number of DevOps topics such as blameless postmortems, ChatOps, and modern incident management. A frequent speaker at DevOps-related events and conferences around the country, Jason enjoys talking to audiences large and small on a variety of technical and non-technical subjects.

CPSIA information can be obtained
at www.ICGtesting.com
Printed in the USA
FSOW04n0123071016
25708FS